The Story of Simone Biles

Rising Above and Redefining Gymnastics

Harper Blackwood

Copyright

Copyright

Disclaimer

The book "Simone Biles: Rising Above and Redefining Gymnastics" provides a thorough overview of the extraordinary path and accomplishments of the gymnastics star. Interviews, firsthand recollections, and publicly accessible data served as the foundation for this book. It aims to give a truthful and uplifting overview of her life and work. Although every effort has been taken to assure accuracy, there is a possibility that certain facts will alter in the future. The goal of the book is to commemorate and emphasize Simone Biles's remarkable accomplishments and significance, rather than to present an extensive or definitive biography. The author's opinions and views are presented in this book; they may not represent Simone Biles, her family, or her representatives.

Table Of Contents

Introduction

With an unprecedented 38 Olympic and World Championship medals, Simone Biles holds the record for being the most decorated gymnast in history. After being introduced to gymnastics at the age of six, Biles rapidly rose to prominence in the junior elite division before launching into the senior elite ranks with great fanfare. When she won the all-around crowns at the 2013 World and U.S. Championships, she became a formidable force in the sport, and her career took off. Ever since, Biles has broken numerous records, including nine all-around U.S.

Championship crowns and six all-around World titles.

She won five gold at the 2016 Rio Olympics thanks to her amazing performances, cementeding her place in gymnastics history. Biles courageously withdrew from multiple events at the 2020 Tokyo Olympics to prioritize her mental health in face of extreme pressure, and she still managed to win two medals. She triumphantly returned to competition in August 2023 after a two-year break, and she is currently enthralling spectators once again at the 2024 Summer Olympics in Paris, where she was crucial to the United States winning team gold.

In addition to her accomplishments in gymnastics, Biles is well-known for her personal life. Her inspirational narrative is further enhanced by the fact that she is married to NFL player Jonathan Owens. Biles' journey is a monument to her tenacity, devotion, and unbreakable spirit; it's not just about the medals and records.

Chapter One

Early Life and Family

Simone Biles, a gymnastics legend, was born on March 14, 1997, in Columbus, Ohio. Her early life, filled with hardships and fortitude, laid the groundwork for a journey that would eventually change the sport of gymnastics. Simone was raised in a difficult family situation, and her tale is one of overcoming adversity and finding strength in unexpected places.

Simone's real mother, Shannon Biles, suffered from substance abuse issues, creating an unstable home situation for Simone and her siblings. Recognizing the gravity of the situation, child welfare agencies intervened and placed Simone and her siblings in foster care. This change signaled the start of a new chapter in her life, one marked by uncertainty but with the promise of a greater future.

The Biles siblings soon split up, but Simone and her younger sister, Adria, were taken in by their maternal grandfather, Ron Biles, and his second wife, Nellie. Ron and Nellie Biles lived in Spring, Texas, and provided the daughters with a stable and supportive atmosphere that was critical to their growth. Ron and Nellie formally adopted Simone and Adria in 2003, providing them with not just a safe home, but also the love and support they had missed in their earlier years.

Nellie Biles, a nurse by profession, was especially crucial in Simone's life. Her approach to parenting was based on discipline and encouragement, instilling in Simone the virtues of hard work and determination. This encouraging environment encouraged Simone to pursue her interests, which led her to gymnastics—a discipline that would become her passion and career.

Simone first learned about gymnastics when she was six years old, on a daycare field trip to a gymnastics center. The active and inquisitive young girl was immediately drawn to the sport's acrobatics and precision. The coaches noticed Simone's innate talent and pushed her to pursue gymnastics more seriously. Nellie recognized Simone's promise and enrolled her in a neighborhood gym, where her talent flourished.

As Simone progressed through gymnastics, it became clear that she possessed amazing ability. Her inherent power, agility, and fearless approach to new talents distinguished her from her colleagues. The gym immediately became Simone's second home, a place where she could channel her energy and express her creativity.

Her coaches were astounded by her rapid development and ability to learn complex movements with ease.

Nellie Biles was instrumental in helping Simone advance her gymnastics career. She made sure Simone's training was in balance with her studies and overall well-being. Nellie, who had previously been unaware of the complexities of gymnastics, learned more about the sport to better encourage her kid. She became Simone's advocate, guiding her through the obstacles of a young athlete's life, from juggling education to dealing with the physical demands of rigorous training.

Despite the wonderful environment at home, Simone encountered difficulties outside of it.

Growing up as a young African American girl in a largely white sport, she felt the weight of her differences. There were times when Simone felt alienated or misunderstood, but her ambition never faltered. Simone's family, notably her mother Nellie, provided unflinching support, supporting the conviction that she could accomplish anything she set her mind to.

Simone's progress in gymnastics was swift. By the age of eight, she was already competing at a high level, demonstrating extraordinary skill and poise for her age. Her family recognized the necessity of providing the greatest possible training, so Simone began working with some of the country's top instructors. She improved her talents under their tutelage, eventually establishing a distinct style that combined power and grace.

Simone's love of gymnastics grew stronger with age. Her family remained her most ardent supporters, attending events and celebrating her victories. They also assisted her in overcoming setbacks like as injury and the unavoidable hardships of an elite athletic career. Simone remained grounded throughout, thanks to the firm foundation provided by her family.

Nellie and Ron Biles' support extended beyond the gymnastics competition. They emphasized the importance of education and personal development to ensure Simone's full growth. They encouraged her to pursue interests outside of gymnastics, resulting in a well-rounded individual who was equally comfortable in the classroom as she was on the gym floor.

Simone's early years were characterized by a deep feeling of spirituality and community. The Biles were fervent Christians, and their faith played an important role in their lives. This spiritual basis gave Simone a feeling of purpose and tenacity, allowing her to negotiate the ups and downs of her path. It was a source of strength that supplemented the physical and mental tenacity she gained from gymnastics.

Simone's gymnastics potential became clear as she approached adolescence. She began her training at Bannon's Gymnastix, where she met coach Aimee Boorman. This cooperation would be extremely beneficial to Simone's career.

Aimee noticed Simone's special abilities and worked relentlessly to help her realize her full potential. Simone's talents improved quickly under Aimee's tutelage, and she began to establish herself in the gymnastics scene.

Simone thrived thanks to the support she received from her family and coach. However, the journey was not without its hurdles. The hard training routine, along with the stresses of competition, required a high level of dedication and perseverance. Simone experienced injuries and times of self-doubt, but her family was always there to cheer her up. Their praise and belief in her ability provided ongoing drive.

Simone Biles' early childhood and family tale tells of overcoming adversity, finding strength in the community, and discovering a passion that would change her life forever. Her journey from a difficult childhood to becoming a gymnastics prodigy exemplifies the strength of resilience and the value of a nurturing environment. Simone's family was important in shaping her into the athlete and person she is today, giving the basis on which she built her incredible career.

As Simone grew and excelled, her tale inspired many others. She smashed down barriers and established new standards in gymnastics, not just with her extraordinary abilities, but also with her composure and character. Her family instilled in her the principles of hard labor, tenacity, and faith, which remained important to her identity and guided her through the obstacles and successes of her career.

Simone Biles' early life and family background are essential for knowing the person behind the gymnast. They reveal the source of her amazing dedication and resilience, which have propelled her to the top of her sport. Her story is a strong reminder of the importance of a loving and supporting family, and how, with the right foundation, even the most formidable hurdles can be overcome to reach greatness.

Simone's narrative would continue to unfold in extraordinary ways over the years, with her family by her side at all times. Their steadfast support and love have been a continual source of strength for Simone, guiding her through the highs and lows of her journey. As she prepares for future challenges and possibilities, the skills she received from her early life and family will serve her well, both on and off the gymnastics floor.

Simone Biles' early childhood exemplifies the strength of the human spirit and the need of a loving family. It's a narrative about overcoming adversity, discovering one's passion, and relentless pursuit of perfection. Simone's story continues to inspire people all across the world, reminding them that with determination and support, everything is possible.

Chapter Two

The Start of a Gymnastics Journey

Simone Biles' journey into gymnastics began in an unexpected place: a daycare field trip to Bannon's Gymnastix. Simone was only six years old in 2003. According to the narrative, little Biles was intrigued by the athletes' flips and tumbling. She instinctively mirrored their gestures, drawing the attention of the teachers. They were so taken with her inherent talent and passion that they sent a note home recommending she enroll in gymnastics classes. This moment signaled the start of what would be a remarkable journey in the sport.

Simone rapidly displayed a level of talent that separated her apart from her contemporaries while being coached by Aimee Boorman. Boorman, who would eventually coach Simone for most of her competitive career, saw the young gymnast's potential. Simone has a rare combination of power, quickness, and a daring attitude toward mastering new talents. Her early training at Bannon's Gymnastix was demanding, and Simone soon rose through the ranks.

As Simone advanced, it became evident that she was more than just another talented gymnast. Her physical abilities were remarkable. Standing 4 feet 8 inches tall, her compact, muscular physique offered her an advantage in producing the strength required for the explosive maneuvers that would become her signature. This strength, paired with her suppleness and body awareness, enabled her to do skills beyond the grasp of most gymnasts her age.

Simone's first taste of real competition occurred when she began competing in junior elite contests. At 14, she competed in the American Classic, a crucial event for gymnasts hoping to advance to higher-level competitions. Despite her youth and inexperience, Simone finished third in the all-around competition, indicating her presence on the national stage. This performance was only the beginning of her meteoric rise.

Simone made her debut at the United States Classic in 2011, which is another important event for gymnasts seeking to elite classification. She demonstrated her developing skills on all four apparatuses: vault, uneven bars, balancing beam, and floor exercise. Her performances were not only technically hard, but she did them with polish and confidence that belied her age. That year, she finished 20th in the all-around at the USA Gymnastics National Championships, which was an impressive performance for a novice. Simone was clearly learning the sport's nuances and on track for even greater success.

Simone's breakthrough came the next year, in 2012. She competed in numerous big tournaments, including the U.S. Classic and the National Championships, where her efforts drew widespread attention. She won the all-around at the U.S. Classic, demonstrating her overall ability. This triumph marked a watershed moment in her career, establishing her as a prominent competitor in American gymnastics. It also demonstrated her versatility and consistency across all apparatuses, establishing her as a formidable all-around competitor.

Simone's trip was not without hurdles. In 2012, she suffered a big setback as a result of a growth spurt that impaired her training and balance. This time of transition tested her resilience and adaptability. Simone worked extensively with her coaches to re-calibrate her routines, adapting her approaches to fit her evolving body. This event taught her vital lessons about patience and the significance of adapting to situations beyond her control.

Despite these hurdles, Simone's results improved. By 2013, she was prepared to participate on the international arena. Her debut at the American Cup, an international invitational meet, marked a watershed moment in her career. Simone performed admirably against some of the world's top gymnasts, earning second in the all-around. This performance served as a prelude to her participation in the World Championships later that year.

At the 2013 World Championships in Antwerp, Belgium, Simone made history. She became the first African American woman to win the World Championship all-around title. Her performances were nothing less than outstanding. On the floor exercise, she impressed the judges and the crowd with her powerful tumbling and expressive choreography, getting one of the best ratings in the competition. Her vaults were equally outstanding, with difficult feats carried out with accuracy and control. Simone's triumph in Antwerp was a result of her hard work, skill, and the backing of her coaching staff.

Simone's achievement in the World Championships not only cemented her status as a top figure in gymnastics, but also marked the start of a period of dominance in the sport. She kept pushing the boundaries of what was possible in gymnastics, continuously challenging herself to acquire new talents and improve her techniques. Her routines were notoriously challenging, with many components that were unique to her. This includes the "Biles" on the floor exercise—a double layout with a half twist—and the "Biles" on the balance beam, which is a double-twisting double backflip dismount. These talents, named after her, became icons of her creativity and prowess.

Simone's family was instrumental in her early professional success. Her parents, Ron and Nellie Biles, were staunch in their support, providing both financial and emotional encouragement. They helped Simone strike a healthy balance between her gymnastics profession and her personal life, emphasizing the value of education and self-care. This support network was critical as Simone negotiated the challenges of competitive gymnastics and the public scrutiny that accompanied her burgeoning celebrity.

Simone's rise in gymnastics was also characterized by her distinct approach to competition. She was well-known for her contagious enthusiasm and pleasant attitude, and she was frequently seen smiling and talking warmly with her competitors. This manner disguised the intense competitor beneath. Simone's mental toughness was crucial to her success, helping her to remain focused and composed under the severe strain of international competition. Her ability to perform regularly at the top level was due to not just her physical abilities, but also her extensive psychological preparation.

Simone's continuing success made her a role model for young athletes around the world. Her path from a little child discovering gymnastics to a world champion was amazing, proving that with hard work, devotion, and support, anything is possible. Simone's narrative struck a chord with many people, particularly young African

American girls, who saw her as a reflection of themselves and an inspiration.

By the end of her early career, Simone Biles had solidified her position as a dominant force in gymnastics. Her efforts were not only about winning gold, but also about moving the sport ahead. She had redefined what was possible, establishing new benchmarks for complexity and execution. Her impact went beyond the gym, as she used her platform to advocate for critical causes such as mental health and racial equality.

Chapter Three

The Breakthrough Years

Simone Biles' rise to become one of the greatest gymnasts of all time was marked by a series of watershed moments that not only demonstrated her enormous talent but also transformed the sport. The term "The Breakthrough Years" refers to the critical phase in her career when she went from a promising young gymnast to a dominant force on the international scene.

Simone's early gymnastics career hinted at her potential, but it wasn't until she began competing at the national and international levels that her amazing abilities were revealed. The first phase of her breakout occurred during the 2011 and 2012 seasons, when she began to build a name for herself among the junior elite. Her performances were distinguished by a unique blend of strength, precision, and an instinctive sense of artistry, setting her apart from her colleagues. During these years, the gymnastics community began to appreciate her unusual combination of strength and grace in the sport.

Simone, on the other hand, genuinely burst onto the international scene in 2013. This year represented her first major breakthrough, when she competed at the World Championships in Antwerp, Belgium. She was only 16 years old and faced tremendous pressure and competition, yet her performances exceeded expectations. Simone not only won the all-around championship, becoming the first African American woman to do so, but she also won gold in floor exercise and silver in vault. Her all-around victory demonstrated her consistency and adaptability on all apparatuses, a trait that would define her career.

Simone's victory at the 2013 World Championships marked a watershed moment for both her and the sport. Her routines were not only technically outstanding, but they also included novel aspects that pushed the limits of what was thought feasible in women's gymnastics. The force and difficulty of her skills, mixed with her captivating appearance, attracted both crowds and judges. It was around this period that the moniker "Biles" became connected with pioneering abilities, a trend that would last throughout her career.

The following year, 2014, confirmed Simone's position as a dominant force in gymnastics. At the World Championships in Nanning, China, she successfully defended her all-around title. This victory gave her the first woman to win two World all-around titles in a row since Svetlana Khorkina in 2001 and 2003. In addition to her overall performance, Simone won gold medals in balancing beam and floor exercise, demonstrating her skill and adaptability.

Simone stood out during these breakthrough years not only for her ability to win, but also for how she won. Her performances were packed with unparalleled complexity, but she performed them with accuracy and confidence that belied her childhood. The gymnastics world was impressed by her ability to combine force, elegance, and an apparently fearless approach to competition. Her exploits were more than just about winning gold; they were also about setting new standards and motivating future generations of gymnasts.

Simone's supremacy extended into 2015, a year that solidified her legend. She accomplished an incredible achievement in the World Championships in Glasgow, Scotland, by winning her third consecutive all-around title, a modern-day gymnastics record. This accomplishment demonstrated her constancy and unrelenting commitment to greatness. In addition to her all-around victory, Simone won gold in floor exercise and balancing beam, and bronze in vault. Her performance in Glasgow was a masterclass in competitive gymnastics, demonstrating her ability to execute under pressure and produce when it was most important.

During these breakthrough years, Simone not only won an impressive number of medals, but she also brought various new components to the sport, many of which now retain her name. The

"Biles" on floor exercise, a double layout half-out, and the "Biles" on vault, a Yurchenko half-on, double twist off, are just a few of the techniques she developed. These components demonstrate her unique approach to gymnastics and ambition to advance the sport. Her ability to continually introduce new and difficult abilities distinguishes her as a pioneer and inventor.

Simone's performances during this time were remarkable for their artistry and emotion. Unlike many gymnasts, Simone excelled at combining strength and grace. Her floor routines were particularly notable, combining intricate tumbling passes with expressive choreography that kept viewers captivated. Her ability to convey a story via her routines provided depth to her performances, making them not just technically outstanding but also visually appealing.

The significance of Simone's breakthrough years went beyond her individual accomplishments. She became a symbol of brilliance and endurance, motivating numerous young gymnasts to follow their goals. Her tale resonated with people all throughout the world, especially those from underprivileged groups. As the first African American woman to attain such dominance in gymnastics, Simone defied prejudices and demonstrated that skill and hard effort can overcome any impediment.

Furthermore, Simone's influence extended beyond the sport of gymnastics. She became a cultural figure, revered for her dedication, modesty, and fortitude. Her story of overcoming difficulties, which included negotiating the pressures of being in the public eye and dealing with personal issues, struck a chord with a wide audience. Simone's candor about her experiences, particularly her mental health issues, sparked crucial discussions about athletes' well-being and the demands they confront.

As the gymnastics world saw Simone Biles climb to popularity during these breakthrough years, it became evident that she was not only a great athlete, but also a game-changing personality in the sport. Her mix of technique, originality, and personality established a new standard of excellence and inspired a new generation of gymnasts to aspire for greatness.

Her breakout years are remembered not only for the medals she earned, but also for the indelible impact she left on gymnastics, which will continue to inspire and influence the sport for many years to come.

Simone Biles' breakout years were a time of incredible accomplishment and growth. Her journey from a young gymnast with enormous promise to a global symbol of the sport is one of perseverance, invention, and achievement. As she continues to compete and inspire, her status as one of history's greatest gymnasts is cemented, and her impact on the sport and beyond is unmistakable. Simone Biles' tale is more than just gymnastics; it is about breaking down boundaries, challenging limitations, and redefining what is possible.

Chapter Four

Dominance on the World Stage

Simone Biles' road to becoming a dominant force in gymnastics on a global scale is one of unrivaled devotion, resilience, and exceptional talent. Biles demonstrated promise as a young athlete, but it was her unique blend of athleticism, precision, and mental toughness that distinguished her from hver colleagues and propelled her to change the sport.

Simone Biles rose to prominence on the international stage with a rare combination of force and finesse in gymnastics. Her routines were of exceptional difficulty, exhibiting elements that few other gymnasts dared to attempt. This daring approach rapidly established her as a leader in the sport. Her ability to execute intricate maneuvers with seeming ease not only set new marks, but also broadened gymnastics' possibilities. Biles' routines were a display of athleticism, blending high-flying leaps with precise, delicate movements.

Her domination extended beyond the technical aspects of the sport. Biles had an unusual capacity to handle pressure, which became more apparent as she continued to compete at the highest levels. Her calm manner and unwavering focus during competitions demonstrated her mental fortitude, allowing her to perform consistently even under the most intense pressure. This mental fortitude was especially important in high-stakes circumstances, where the margin for error was small and the expectations were high.

Biles' success did not happen immediately. It was the culmination of years of tough preparation and an unwavering dedication to greatness. Her training schedule was rigorous, requiring many hours of practice and precise attention to detail. Every routine was meticulously planned, with Biles and her coaches constantly pushing the limits of what she could accomplish. This constant quest of perfection was evident in her performances, where even little errors were uncommon.

One of Biles' defining moments occurred at the 2013 World Championships in Antwerp, Belgium. This was her first major international tournament, and she did not disappoint. Biles put on a series of amazing performances, demonstrating her outstanding abilities and winning her first two world championship championships in the all-around and floor exercise categories. This victory established her as a force to be reckoned with, laying the groundwork for her sustained domination in the years to come.

Following her breakthrough in 2013, Biles continued to push the limits of the sport. She became well-known for her inventive routines, which frequently featured aspects that were previously deemed too difficult or risky. Her signature move, the "Biles," demonstrates her ingenuity and bravery. The maneuver, a double layout with a half twist, is so difficult that only a few gymnasts have attempted it in competition. By continuously including such challenging aspects into her routines, Biles not only demonstrated her remarkable talent, but also inspired other gymnasts to improve their own performances.

Biles' supremacy was reinforced at the 2014 and 2015 World Championships. She continued to win titles, becoming the first woman to win three straight all-around world championships. Her performances were distinguished by a degree of complexity and execution that set her apart from her competitors. In addition to her all-around crowns, Biles won gold medals in vault, balancing beam, and floor exercise. Her versatility and ability to excel in various disciplines cemented her reputation as a complete gymnast.

The Rio 2016 Olympics were another high point in Biles' career. As the face of the United States women's gymnastics team, she had high expectations for the Games. Biles once again rose to the occasion, delivering a sequence of performances that astounded both audiences and judges. She earned four gold medals and one bronze, establishing her place among the best gymnasts of all time. Her success in Rio was the result of years of hard work, determination, and an unwavering pursuit of perfection.

Beyond her technical skill, Biles' performances were distinguished by an air of elegance and grace that charmed viewers all over the world. Her performances were not only a showcase of athleticism, but also a form of artistic expression. Biles' ability to blend strength and elegance, power and precision, made her performances enjoyable to watch. She had an incredible ability to connect with the audience, bringing them into her acts and having them feel the emotions she was expressing.

While Biles' dominance in the sport is unquestionable, her path was not without obstacles. She endured injuries and setbacks, putting her resolve and commitment to the test. However, each challenge seemed to reinforce her resolve. Biles' resilience in the face of hardship is an important part of her story. She has often demonstrated that she possesses both the physical ability and the mental courage required to overcome obstacles and emerge stronger.

Biles' impact goes beyond her individual successes. She has served as a role model and inspiration to innumerable young gymnasts around the world. Her narrative is about breaking barriers and pushing the boundaries of what is possible. She has demonstrated that hard effort, perseverance, and a bold approach can lead to greatness. Biles' success has also boosted awareness of the sport of gymnastics, inspiring a new generation of competitors to follow their goals.

In addition to her athletic accomplishments, Biles has used her platform to promote significant social causes. She has spoken out on the need for more athlete support and protection, particularly in light of recent disclosures of abuse in the sport. Biles' courage to speak out on these matters has drawn much-needed attention to the challenges that athletes confront, as well as generated vital discussions about sports safety and accountability.

As Biles continued to compete and dominate on the global stage, she never lost sight of the love and enthusiasm that drew her to the sport in the first place. Her love for gymnastics shines through in every performance, and her energy is contagious. This enthusiasm, along with her extraordinary talent, has made Biles not only a champion, but also a revered figure in the sporting world.

Chapter Five

The Road to the 2016 Olympics

On August 9, 2016, Simone Biles led the United States women's gymnastics team to a historic gold medal win at the Rio Olympics. Her performances were nothing less than outstanding. Biles scored an astounding 15.933 in the vault, demonstrating her remarkable power and technique. On the balancing beam, she earned 15.3, exhibiting her exceptional balance and control. The highlight, however, was her popular floor act, which earned her a 15.8. This routine featured her signature move, the Biles, a double layout flip with a half twist that wowed the audience and judges. Biles celebrated this historic victory alongside her teammates Gabby Douglas, Laurie Hernandez,

Madison Kocian, and Aly Raisman. They were collectively known as "The Final Five."

The moniker "The Final Five" had unique importance. Raisman emphasized its significance on the Today Show, saying, "We're the Final Five because this is [coach] Marta [Karolyi's] final Olympics, and none of this would have been possible... We wanted to do it for her simply because she is with us every day. She also mentioned another reason: "This is the last Olympics with a five-woman squad. "The next Olympics will only feature a four-person team." This gave emotional and historical significance to their victory.

The Final Five's victory in Rio was the third time an American women's gymnastics team had won gold, after 1996 and 2012. Biles brilliantly expressed the team's thoughts with her tweet following their victory: "dreams DO come true," accompanied by a photo of the US team on the medal podium. The image of Aly Raisman, Madison Kocian, Laurie Hernandez, Gabby Douglas, and Simone Biles standing together, each wearing a gold Olympic medal and pointing one finger into the air, has become legendary. They were dressed in navy blue and red Team USA sweatshirts, and their faces were bright as they celebrated their hard-earned victory.

Biles' dominance went beyond the team events. In the women's individual all-around competition, she won gold with a final score of 62.198. This score put her 2.1 points ahead of silver medalist Aly Raisman, setting an unprecedented margin of victory. Biles' lead over her competitors was higher than any gymnast's margin of victory between 1980 and 2012. Her all-around victory cemented her place as a gymnastics superstar, making her the first woman in two decades to win the Olympic all-around and World titles back-to-back.

Her achievements included a gold medal in the vault, when she achieved 15.966. This event showcased her tremendous power and impeccable execution. However, it was not without difficulties. Biles got a bronze medal on the balancing beam with a score of 14.733. During this routine, she had a rare stumble and struggled to keep her balance. Despite this, she reflected on her performance with determination, telling USA Today, "The rest of the routine was still pretty good, so I can't be too disappointed in myself."

Biles' Olympic victory concluded with her floor exercise. She gave an outstanding performance, garnering 15.966 points and securing yet another gold medal. This performance, which featured her hallmark move, the Biles, demonstrated her outstanding brilliance and artistry in gymnastics.

Biles won five medals at the Rio Olympics, including four golds and one bronze. Her extraordinary feat elevated her to the ranks of elite gymnasts. She joined the ranks of Larisa Latynina of the Soviet Union in 1956, Vera Caslavska of Czechoslovakia in 1968, and Ecaterina Szabo of Romania in 1984, all of whom won four gold medals in a single Olympics. Biles' achievements not only demonstrated her tremendous skill and dedication, but also secured her position as one of the best gymnasts of all time.

Chapter Six

Record-Breaking Performances at the U.S. Nationals and World Championships

After missing much of 2017, Simone Biles returned triumphantly to competitive gymnastics, reinforcing her status as the sport's most powerful force. Her comeback began in 2018 at the United States Gymnastics Championships, where she gave a remarkable performance that proved her dominance. Biles won all four events—vault, uneven bars, balancing beam, and floor exercise—for a total score that surpassed her nearest opponent by an astounding 6.55 points. This victory made her the first woman to win five national all-around medals, demonstrating her exceptional skill and consistency.

Biles did not stop there; she continued to push the frontiers of gymnastics. In 2019, she became the first gymnast to perform a double-double dismount off the balancing beam, which consists of two flips and two twists. This was once thought to be nearly impossible due to the enormous complexity and precision required. But Biles, ever the innovator, made it appear practically effortless. Her performance at the U.S. Nationals that year demonstrated her great talent and relentless drive to develop. She was also the first woman to complete a triple-double in the floor exercise, which is a demanding series of three twists and two flips that requires exceptional aerial awareness and control.

These game-changing moves symbolized Biles' never-ending ambition to elevate the sport. By performing something no woman had done before, she pushed the boundaries of gymnastics and set new benchmarks for future generations. Her sixth U.S. Nationals victory in 2019 was practically inevitable, considering her unrivaled powers and the gap she had created between herself and her competitors.

The 2019 World Championships in Stuttgart, Germany, solidified Biles' position as the greatest gymnast of all time. She won her fifth individual all-around gold medal, raising her total World Championship medal count to a record-breaking 25. This feat broke the previous record held by Belarusian gymnast Vitaly Scherbo, becoming Biles the most decorated athlete in World Championship history. Her gymnastics routines were brilliant, combining technical proficiency, agility, and beauty in a way that few others could match. Each event saw her do acts with unrivaled difficulty, stunning crowds and judges.

Biles' supremacy on the international stage continued in 2021, when she made headlines once more at the GK US Classic in Indianapolis. On May 22, she became the first female to successfully land the Yurchenko double pike in competition. This technique, primarily executed by male gymnasts, begins with a roundoff onto the springboard, followed by a back handspring onto the vault, and ends with a piked double backflip for the landing. The Yurchenko double pike is an extremely difficult skill that requires a high level of strength, precision, and daring. Biles' successful execution of the move was more than a personal accomplishment; it was a watershed moment in gymnastics history. It demonstrated her outstanding ability and desire to push the boundaries, testing both herself and the sport's conventions.

The Yurchenko double pike, which has become synonymous with Biles, was a highlight of her 2021 performances. She executed the technique well at the 2023 U.S. Classic, U.S. Gymnastics Championships, and World Artistic Gymnastics Championships. The latter case was especially noteworthy because it was the first time a female gymnast performed the skill at an international competition. This accomplishment resulted in the move being nicknamed the "Biles," further honoring her achievements to the sport. Naming a move after a gymnast is one of the sport's highest accolades, recognizing both the athlete's uniqueness and the historical significance of their feat.

Biles' career is distinguished not just by her competitive accomplishments, but also by her status as a trailblazer and innovator. Her determination to try and achieve techniques that others consider unattainable has established a new standard for gymnastics. She has continuously advanced the sport, not only by smashing records but also by rethinking the limits of what gymnasts can accomplish. Her effect goes beyond her technical abilities; she has become a symbol of tenacity, fortitude, and grace under pressure.

Biles has experienced numerous hurdles during her career, both on and off the mat. Nonetheless, her capacity to overcome these challenges and continue to perform at the highest level demonstrates her amazing character. Her accomplishments in the US Nationals and World Championships demonstrate her passion to her art and unwavering pursuit of excellence. Biles' legacy is not only the records she has broken or the medals she has won, but also the motivation she brings to athletes all around the world. She has demonstrated that hard effort, determination, and a willingness to take risks can lead to greatness.

To summarize, Simone Biles' results at the US Nationals and World Championships were nothing short of revolutionary. She has not only broken records, but also pushed the bounds of gymnastics by introducing new skills and redefining what is possible in the sport. Her accomplishments have elevated her to the ranks of history's best athletes, and her legacy will continue to inspire future generations of gymnasts. Whether performing a double-double dismount or landing the Yurchenko double pike, Biles continuously displays why she is regarded as the greatest gymnast in history. Her journey demonstrates the power of tenacity, ingenuity, and a relentless pursuit of perfection.

Chapter Seven

2020 Olympic Games Withdrawal

The run-up to Simone Biles's second Olympic performance was full of expectations. Biles had already raised the standard for herself and her sport to an extraordinary level as one of the most decorated gymnasts in history. Her selection to the U.S. Olympic team in June 2021, before the 2020 Tokyo Olympics were postponed, came as no surprise. But these Olympics turned out to be very different from her last one, highlighting the challenges of competing at such a high level in unheard-of conditions.

The entire world was waiting anxiously for Biles to dominate the gymnastics events as she had in the past as the Tokyo Olympics drew near. But something unexpected occurred throughout the competition. In gymnastics, Biles encountered a condition known as "the twisties," which is a frightening and disorienting state in which a gymnast loses consciousness of their own space while in midair. Given that the chance of harm is greatly increased, this condition may be risky. Recognizing the seriousness of the situation, Biles made the painful choice—which stunned both the athletic community and fans—to withdraw from the women's team gymnastics final.

After her withdrawal, Biles spoke openly about her choice and emphasized the value of mental health in a news conference. "It's important to prioritize mental health," she said. "Because you won't enjoy your sport as much and you won't succeed as much as you want to if you don't." Her remarks struck a deep chord and brought attention to a crucial topic that athletes frequently deal with but seldom bring up in public: the psychological and emotional strain of competitive excellence.

Team USA was immediately impacted by Biles's absence. The squad had to reorganize and adjust fast without their star gymnast. They faced difficulties, but they still performed admirably and won a silver medal. Although commendable, this accomplishment served as a reminder of the intense pressure and high risks associated with competing in the Olympics. Suni Lee and other Biles teammates filled in for her. Lee's remarkable talent and tenacity were demonstrated when she went on to win the individual all-around championship. In addition to being a personal victory for Lee, this result demonstrated the caliber of skill in American gymnastics.

The Olympics in Tokyo were a turning moment in Biles' life. She made the decision to withdraw from the individual all-around competition as well as the vault, uneven bars, and floor exercise finals. She returned, nevertheless, for the balance beam final, where she performed admirably and took home a bronze medal with a score of 14.000. This was a pivotal moment that showed her bravery and will to fight for what she wanted. Although it wasn't her greatest achievement, the bronze medal served as a potent representation of tenacity and fortitude.

Biles shared her experience with the twisties in an April 2024 audio interview with Call Her Daddy. She spoke of the illness as a terrifying and unsettling experience when she felt as though her body and mind weren't working together. She said, "It was as though I was fighting my body to perform these tricks." "Your brain opens up, just like your body does, and you have no idea where you are." Her open talk highlighted the frequently disregarded mental health issues that athletes deal with, especially in high-stress settings like the Olympics.

It was revolutionary for Biles to put her mental health before sport. It contradicted the widely held belief that athletes must overcome all obstacles, both mental and physical. Her actions spurred a more general discussion on the value of mental health in athletics and other contexts. Biles developed into a well-known mental health champion, use her position to inspire people to get care when they need it.

After the Olympics in Tokyo, Biles took a long hiatus from competing. She joined treatment, prioritized her mental health, and practiced self-care during this period. She was able to prioritize her mental and emotional health and reflect on her experiences, which was essential for her rehabilitation and overall wellbeing. Numerous others have been encouraged to treat their mental health seriously by Biles' candidness about her challenges and proactive attitude to it.

Even though it was difficult, the Olympics in Tokyo brought attention to Biles' significant influence on gymnastics as well as her pioneering role. A new benchmark for athletes was set by her willingness to be transparent about her challenges and make tough choices for her own wellbeing. By demonstrating that it is possible to prioritize one's mental health in addition to being an outstanding athlete, Biles challenged the stigma that is frequently attached to mental health difficulties in athletics.

The Olympics in Tokyo served as a poignant reminder of athletes' humanity through Simone Biles' experience. It emphasized the value of resilience, mental health, and having the guts to make tough choices when faced with hardship. Even though she did not have the flawless, gold-medal performance that many had hoped for, it was still a significant and influential period in her career. In addition to being one of the greatest gymnasts of all time, Simone Biles became a role model for self-care and mental health awareness after the Olympics in Tokyo.

As Biles travels further, her time in Tokyo continues to be significant. It is evidence of her mental and physical toughness as well as her steadfast dedication to her health. Her narrative inspires athletes and people all around the world, serving as a constant reminder of the value of putting one's mental health first and the bravery required to put oneself first.

Chapter Seven

Return to Competition

It was nothing short of spectacular when Simone Biles triumphantly returned to competition gymnastics in 2023. She returned to competition at the early August 2023 Core Hydration Classic, formerly the U.S. Classic, following a two-year hiatus from the sport. Fans and other competitors couldn't have been more excited about her comeback, wondering if the legendary gymnast could still rule the sport. Along with taking first place in the floor and beam events, Biles not only met but surpassed these expectations by winning the all-around title by an incredible 5 points.

Her winning performance in the Core Hydration Classic demonstrated her unmatched skill and readiness. Biles maintained the same level of focus, strength, and grace that had characterized her career throughout her break. The crowd and judges were in complete awe of her performances because of their extreme complexity and faultless execution. After winning, Biles said she was happy with her performance and said she felt "really good about where I am right now, physically and mentally." Although I still believe there is room for improvement in my routines, I would say that the first match back went really well. I'm really taken aback and startled." Even after such a commanding performance, her humility and dedication to ongoing development demonstrated her unwavering pursuit of excellence.

After winning the Classic, Biles was guaranteed a spot in the U.S. Championships later that month, when she created history once more. She broke the tie with the late Alfred Jochim, who had held seven all-around wins since 1933, to become the first gymnast to win eight national all-around titles. This accomplishment was significant not just because it demonstrated her ongoing excellence over time but also because it highlighted her longevity in a field where younger athletes frequently dominate. Biles accomplished a unique feat that attests to her persistent physical and mental strength: at the age of 26, she became the oldest woman to win a national title.

Biles maintained her reign of terror at the U.S. Championships, taking home gold in both the beam and floor events. She performed with a combination of athleticism, technical proficiency, and complex choreography, each move carried out with a level of expertise that only she could provide. Her routines aimed to captivate the audience with her emotive and self-assured approach in addition to mastering challenging components. Her reputation as the best gymnast of her time and among the most accomplished competitors in the sport's history was cemented at the Championships.

In October, Biles competed internationally for the first time in the past two years, joining Team USA at the 2023 World Artistic Gymnastics Championships after her triumph at the national level. Despite the intense pressure, Biles flourished and helped the American ladies win the world championship seven times in a row. She continuously received top grades in every event, which made her vital to the team's victory. In the all-around, balancing beam, and floor exercise, Biles earned gold medals individually. In the vault, she took home silver. With these triumphs, she surpassed all previous World Championship medal totals and became the most decorated gymnast in history.

Biles's accomplishments at the World Championships served as evidence of her unmatched skill and tenacity. It's an uncommon achievement in any sport for her to be able to dominate even after a lengthy sabbatical and return to the highest levels of competition. Her routines pushed the limits of what is possible in gymnastics, and her performances were distinguished by an amazing blend of difficulty and execution. Her intricate skills, which included the height of her jumps and the accuracy of her landings, distinguished her from her rivals.

Beyond the medals and records, Biles' achievements hold great significance. She is now regarded as a symbol of tenacity and power, encouraging athletes everywhere to keep going in the face of difficulties and disappointments. Her return to sport required not just physical training but also mental toughness. Biles has been transparent about her battles with mental health, especially those brought on by the demands of elite competition. Her choice to take a sabbatical and then resume competition on her own terms has made a strong statement about the value of self-care and mental health.

In addition to her outstanding accomplishments, Simone Biles' legacy is shaped by her influence on the sport and the larger dialogue surrounding athlete wellbeing. Not only has she raised the bar for technical proficiency in gymnastics, but she has also redefined the way gymnasts are supported and cared for. Her support of athlete rights and mental health has spurred significant discussions and improved conditions in the sport.

Biles is still a powerful force and an inspiration to others as she pursues her career. Her legendary position has only grown as a result of her accomplishments at the 2023 World Artistic Gymnastics Championship, the U.S. Championships, and the Core Hydration Classic. She has demonstrated that being the best in gymnastics involves more than just winning—it also involves pushing boundaries, shattering barriers, and motivating other people. Her life narrative is one of tenacity, devotion, and an unwavering quest for excellence, which has made her one of the greatest athletes of all time.

The journey of Simone Biles is far from ended, and her future aspirations in gymnastics and other pursuits will surely never cease to motivate and inspire. Biles is the epitome of excellence and tenacity, whether she is competing, supporting worthy causes, or just being an inspiration to others. Her 2023 comeback to competition served as a reminder of both her tremendous talent and her enduring influence on the sports world.

Chapter Eight

2024 Olympics

Simone Biles continued to establish herself as the best gymnast of all time in the first half of 2024 with incredible feats that showed off her unrivaled talent, tenacity, and love for the sport. Her performance in both the U.S. Championships and the Core Hydration Classic was astounding. Biles won the all-around title at the Core Hydration Classic, demonstrating her amazing talent and demonstrating her continuous supremacy in the sport. This triumph served as a prelude to her incredible showing at the U.S. Championships, where she set a new record with nine victories, solidifying her status as the most decorated gymnast in the history of the competition.

Biles performed technically perfect and artistically compelling routines at the U.S. Championships, which were a masterclass in gymnastics. Both the judges and the audience were in awe of her feats on the uneven bars, vault, balancing beam, and floor exercise. She was pushing the limits of gymnastics with each routine, showcasing her extraordinary skill and precision. Biles's resilience and commitment to her work are evident in her ability to continuously produce top-notch performances even in the face of extreme stress.

Biles' triumph at the U.S. Olympic Team Trials on June 30, 2024, sealed her ticket to the 2024 Summer Olympics in Paris. With this victory, she was guaranteed a position on Team USA, becoming the first American gymnast to qualify for three Olympic teams since 2000. With this incredible accomplishment, she joined a limited group of gymnasts who have already competed in three Olympic Games: Dominique Dawes, Linda Metheny, and Muriel Davis Grossfeld. The fact that Biles made the 2024 squad demonstrated both her tenacity and talent, as well as her capacity to stay at the top of the sport for more than ten years.

Biles got off to a great start at the Paris Games, leading the team all-around qualifying rounds in both the vault and floor exercise. Her incredible exploits gave the United States the best seed going into the championship, which gave the squad more confidence. Biles earned a score of 14.666 for her incredible floor exercise routine in the team all-around final. Her performance, along with those of her colleagues, helped the United States win their fourth gold medal as a team in Olympic history. Biles made a significant contribution, demonstrating her leadership and capacity to execute well under duress on the biggest platform in the world.

As of July 30, 2024, Biles has won a staggering number of medals in gymnastics, a tribute to her extraordinary success. She is the most decorated gymnast in history, having racked up an incredible 105 medals in competition. Eight Olympic medals total, five gold, one silver, and two bronze. Quite a remarkable collection. Biles has won 30 medals at the World Championships, including an incredible 23 golds, four silvers, and three bronzes. She is even more dominant at the U.S. Championships, where she has won 41 medals, including four silver, four bronze, and 33 gold. In addition, Biles has 26 medals from the U.S. Classic, comprising 2 silver, 2 bronze, and 22 gold.

The number of medals Biles has won does not sum up her achievements. In addition, she has created history by being the only female gymnast to win six World titles in the all-around competition. She has won nine consecutive all-around titles at the U.S. Championships, which is another evidence of her supremacy and consistency in the sport. As a junior elite gymnast, Biles has also won two World Challenge Cup crowns and several medals throughout the years, demonstrating her skill at an early age.

Along with her athletic accomplishments, Biles has made a substantial contribution to the sport by developing and demonstrating new abilities. Five gymnastics elements bear her name: two in the vault, two on the floor exercise, and one on the balancing beam. Her ability to push the boundaries of the sport and her creative and technical prowess are demonstrated by her eponymous skills. These routines have not only raised the bar, but they have motivated a new wave of gymnasts to reach even higher goals.

The influence of Biles goes beyond the gym. President Joe Biden awarded her the Presidential Medal of Freedom in July 2022 as a mark of honor. This esteemed honor acknowledged her accomplishments to gymnastics as well as her support of athlete safety and mental wellness. Biles has been an outspoken supporter of significant causes, utilizing her position to spread knowledge and encourage constructive change. She is now recognized as a role model for athletes and people all over the world because of her bravery in speaking out about topics pertaining to mental health and the abuse crisis within USA Gymnastics.

The first half of 2024 has seen Simone Biles carry on with her incredible career. Her achievements as the best gymnast of all time are further evidenced by her triumphs in the Core Hydration Classic, U.S. Championships, and U.S. Olympic Team Trials, in addition to her unforgettable performances at the Paris Games. Her remarkable collection of medals, inventive abilities, and activism endeavors demonstrate not just her prowess in gymnastics but also her significant influence on both the sport and the community. Biles is still an inspiration to the next generation, a shining example of bravery, tenacity, and perfection who personifies what it is to be an Olympic champion.

Chapter Nine

Movies

Simone Biles continued to garner media attention in the first half of 2024, not only because of her remarkable gymnastics accomplishments but also because of her activism and presence in popular culture. Biles's varied path exemplifies her talent, tenacity, and influence both on and off the mat.

Biles partnered with professional dancer Sasha Farber in the 24th season of Dancing with the Stars, which debuted in 2017. Fans were excited to see her on the show because they wanted to see how her grace and athleticism from gymnastics would transition to ballroom dancing. From the beginning, Biles wowed the judges and the crowd with her dancing steps, exhibiting a natural talent for the art combined with her competitive nature and commitment to learning new abilities. She consistently won acclaim and high marks from the judges with technically flawless and emotionally compelling performances.

Biles' time on Dancing with the Stars ended abruptly in the quarterfinals in May 2017, despite her impressive performances. Many were surprised that she was eliminated, considering her popularity and steady high scores. But Biles accepted the outcome with the poise and good sportsmanship that have defined her career. She conveyed her appreciation for the encounter, highlighting how it enabled her to push herself beyond her comfort zone and do new things.

Simone Biles Rising, a four-part documentary series that aired on Netflix on July 17, was based on Biles in 2024. Viewers were given a unique insight into Biles's personal and professional life through the close look at her life that the docuseries offered. The initiative tracked Biles's road toward qualifying for the 2024 Summer

Olympics in Paris while juggling her personal life, mental health journey, and demanding training schedule. The series brought to light Biles's struggles and victories as she got ready for another go at Olympic gold through frank interviews and behind-the-scenes video.

Simone Biles Rising was a compelling story of perseverance and overcoming hardship in addition to being a record of her athletic endeavors. It explored Biles' experience with mental health, illuminating the challenges and demands that come with being a top athlete. As a result of the series' candor and ability to raise awareness of mental health issues, Biles' reputation as a trailblazer and advocate was further cemented.

Being a survivor of Larry Nassar's abuse, Biles's participation in the #MeToo movement is one of the biggest and most personal struggles she has had to face. Biles courageously disclosed on Twitter in January 2018 that she was one of the numerous young ladies who the former USA Gymnastics team doctor had harassed. Nassar received sentences of 25 to 40 years in jail for illegal sexual behavior and 60 years in prison for child pornography. Biles' admission was a pivotal point in the story, elevating her voice above the many women who had come forward to reveal Nassar's abuse pattern spanning decades.

Biles said in her statement, "Please believe me when I say it was a lot harder to first speak those words out loud than it is now to put them on paper." She openly discussed her inner battle, acknowledging that she had been doubting herself for far too long and wondered, "Was I too naive? Was I at fault? She declared through her courageous revelation, "I now know the answers to those questions. No. No, I did not cause it. No, I refuse to take on the blame that Larry Nassar, USAG, and other people deserve."

Biles' bravery in speaking up has had a significant influence on the #MeToo movement as a whole as well as the gymnastics community. Due to her willingness to tell her story, USA Gymnastics has undergone substantial improvements, including more oversight and athlete protection reforms. In addition to encouraging many other survivors to come forward, her work has helped bring about a larger cultural shift in favor of accountability and support for victims of abuse.

Beyond her activism and sports endeavors, Biles's impact may be seen in a number of societal concerns and popular cultural contexts. She has discussed topics like mental health, self-care, and racial equality using her platform. Perceptions of mental health in sports have changed significantly as a result of her candidness about her personal difficulties with mental health, especially during the Tokyo 2020 Olympics when she withdrew from multiple competitions to prioritize her health. Biles has pushed for a more sympathetic and perceptive attitude to athlete welfare and stressed the value of putting one's mental health first.

Simone Biles's journey throughout the first half of 2024 and in the years preceding it demonstrate an incredible fusion of personal development, unwavering activism, and physical brilliance. Despite being outside of her comfort zone, her involvement in Dancing with the Stars demonstrated her adaptability and readiness to take on new challenges. The documentary series Simone Biles Rising provided a personal and motivational glimpse into her life, emphasizing her commitment to gymnastics and her fortitude in the face of difficulty.

Significant changes within the sports world and beyond have resulted from Biles's long-lasting involvement in the #MeToo movement and her support for mental health. Her tale of overcoming hardship shows that real strength comes from having the guts to stand up for what is right and speak out against injustice in addition to physical strength. Biles is still a source of inspiration to the globe as she gets ready for the 2024 Summer Olympics in Paris, demonstrating to everyone that anything is possible if one has perseverance, drive, and a strong commitment to their moral principles.

Her story is a potent reminder of the value of mental health, the strength that comes from being vulnerable, and the influence of using one's position to make a difference. In addition to her accolades and records, Simone Biles' legacy is shaped by her bravery, activism, and constant inspiration to people and athletes worldwide.

Chapter Ten

Husband and Networth

The elite gymnast Simone Biles and the NFL player Jonathan Owens combine to create a powerful duo that is effective on and off the field. Both the couple's personal and professional journeys are motivational. Since announcing their relationship to the world in August 2020, Biles and Owens have enthralled audiences with their shared moments and steadfast support of one another. The proposal that Owens made to Biles in February 2022 was a major turning point in their relationship. The public expressions of love and admiration that accompanied their growing relationship culminated in a lovely way with their engagement.

Biles and Owens were legally married in a civil ceremony on April 21, 2023. Less than a month later, on May 6, a lavish destination wedding in Mexico took place after this private affair. With close relatives and friends in attendance, the idyllic wedding in Mexico was a happy and humorous celebration of their love. The couple's intense love and happiness were evident in the wedding images, which were extensively shared on social media.

Biles and Owens have handled the difficulties of a somewhat remote relationship despite having hard and hectic jobs. After settling in the Houston region for most of her gymnastics career, Biles still resides and trains there. Conversely, Owens has been forced to relocate because of his NFL obligations. Owens was a Wisconsin player for the Green Bay Packers when they were married. As a result, the couple had to spend a lot of time apart and relied on frequent visits and technology to stay in touch.

When Owens inked a two-year deal with the Chicago Bears in March 2024, the pair had to make yet another move. This relocation meant a new city and new difficulties, but it also presented chances for the pair to become stronger as a unit. They have demonstrated incredible resiliency and commitment to one another in spite of the distance. In addition, Biles and Owens are constructing a house in Texas as a testament of their dedication to forging a future together. They will be able to retreat to this house together and take a break from their hectic work schedules.

Their story of love is proof of the strength of understanding and support among one another. Both Biles and Owens are accomplished professionals who have managed to strike a balance between their personal and professional goals. Respect and admiration are the cornerstones of their relationship, and it's clear from the way they talk about and acknowledge each other's accomplishments.

The gymnastics career of Biles is nothing short of remarkable. Her wealth, which as of April 2024 is projected to be approximately $16 million, is a result of both her business sense and her skill on the gymnastics floor. Her impressive performance at the 2016 Olympics led to lucrative sponsorship deals, which account for a large portion of her riches. Upon realizing her celebrity potential, prominent companies such as United Airlines, The Hershey Company, and Oreo signed her for their advertisements. Her influence was increased outside of the sports industry in addition to increasing her net worth as a result of these endorsements.

With $8.5 million in earnings in 2023, Biles ranked tenth among female athletes according to Sportico. Her marketability and the respect she commands in the sports world are demonstrated by the fact that almost all of this money comes from speaking engagements and sponsorships. In order to further solidify her status as an influencer and role model, Biles has used her platform to promote vital subjects like athlete safety and mental health.

Even though he is not as well-known as Biles, Jonathan Owens has advanced far in his NFL career. His career in professional football has been characterized by tenacity and diligence, traits that are reflected in Biles' own narrative. With the Chicago Bears, Owens has embarked on a new chapter in his career, one that is sure to bring both obstacles and opportunity. Biles has been a constant supporter of his throughout his career changes, encouraging him and recognizing his accomplishments.

A deep sense of teamwork permeates their connection. On social media, they frequently provide insights into their lives together, including their workout routines, funny moments, and sincere words of support. These posts demonstrate a strong bond based on respect and common ideals. It is quite amazing how they manage the rigors of their work to support each other's goals.

For the couple, building their new Texas home represents a major accomplishment. It stands for consistency and a common outlook for their future. Together, they have demonstrated their dedication to one another and the strength of their partnership by building a home. They can make memories there, commemorate achievements, and find comfort in the middle of their busy lives.

Jonathan Owens and Simone Biles are the epitome of the modern power couple. Their tale of love combines passion, respect for one another, and common goals. They have persevered through hardships and distance, always managing to encourage and support one another. They know they have one other's complete support as they go on to succeed in their separate industries.

For many, their journey together serves as an inspiration. It demonstrates that love and devotion can triumph despite difficult jobs and distance obstacles. Together, Biles and Owens may accomplish greatness because they are not just champions in their sports but also in life, exemplifying the value of respect and encouragement between teammates. Their tale serves as a lovely reminder that real love knows no boundaries and that a genuine partnership may flourish even in the face of individual success.

Printed by Libri Plureos GmbH in Hamburg,
Germany